LIGHT IN THE DARKNESS

Danielle Christy

ISBN 979-8-88943-991-2 (paperback)
ISBN 979-8-88943-992-9 (digital)

Christian Faith Publishing
832 Park Avenue
Meadville, PA 16335
www.christianfaithpublishing.com

Printed in the United States of America

Contents

PART 1

It's More than Unhappiness

Depression

D—Dark dungeon
E—Exhausting
P—Potential to self-harm
R—Reliving nightmare
E—Emotional
S—Suffering
S—Suicide is only way out
I—Isolate
O—Overwhelmed
N—Not deserving

Black Tunnel

It doesn't end
Black, no light in sight
Dark and lonely
Can't see anywhere out
Cold
Never-ending thoughts
Saying
Not worth it
Can't succeed
Just end it
No one will notice
It's time to say goodbye

Who Cares

Why try
It's better to die

> Others get mad
> Always sad

It doesn't matter
You will just shatter

> You're not good enough
> Life will always be rough

It's just not fair
No one cares

> You don't deserve anything

Don't Deserve

You don't deserve to live
You don't deserve to succeed
You don't deserve the help
You don't deserve love
You don't deserve happiness
You don't deserve friendship
You don't deserve talent
You don't deserve to be worthy
You don't deserve sleep
You don't deserve anything

Panic Attack

Racing heart
Sweaty
Shaky
Blacking out
Can't breathe
Alone
Anywhere
Anytime
No one can help
How can I stop this?

Hiding

Don't let them know
Your racing thoughts
They will judge you
And kick you out
Mental illness is not allowed

In your room
Isolated
Dark and gloomy
Wrapped in blankets
Quiet but the constant thoughts
The depression just won't leave
It always finds me where I am

Side Effects

Isolate
Alone is better
Crying is not okay
Antisocial
Shrinking in size
Eyes are hollow
Exhausted
No more talking
Nightmares
Trapped feelings
Self-harm
Suicide

Why Dream?

Don't bother to dream
You will never succeed
You're not smart
So don't even start

         You know you're not good enough
            Others are so tough

You just die anyway
You know you can

Mask

Keep your mask on
Hold it all in
Don't show them the truth
Or they will walk away
Show them the happiness
So they never know
Keep that smile up
The mask only comes off when you're alone

Racing Thoughts

Which way do I go?
How do I know it's right?
Will I succeed?
Why do others care?
What did I do to deserve this?

I'm not worthy
I'm just a burden
No one loves me
I can't
Not strong enough to hold on
Letting others down consistently
Can't have this problem
Can't let others know

Just say goodbye; it's time to go

Fear

Fear will hide inside
Fear is the friend
Fear is the only one
Fear keeps you grounded
Fear will save you from mistakes
Fear will always win

Strong

You have to be strong
Everyone depends on you
Don't let the guard down
Mental illness is not okay
You have to get over it
Stop having this problem
Ignore it

Devil or Truth

What is the truth?

The devil says me
But someone once said "You are worthy"

How do I decide what to do?
Should I just let go?

The devil is right
But I can't let others down
What do I do?

The devil is the only one that's always been there
I guess it's time to listen to it

I have finally made my choice

Suicide

It's time
Choose the method wisely
Make sure to hide
Don't tell anyone
Don't plan, or they'll stop you
Just do it now
Finally let it all go
You will be happy
You know you don't deserve to live
It's time to die

Knife

Grab the knife
On the bathroom floor
Leave the last words on the page
Finally let it all go
Slice the skin
See the blood
Release the pain
The last breath is here
It is done

Unsuccessful

Suicide attempt failed

Everyone will know

Can't deny the problem

Just let me go

Now in the hospital

How can I survive it

Don't want to face it

I can't change

Hospital Experience

Group therapy
Other crazies like me
Medications
Strict routines
Watchful eyes always
Locked in like a jail
Must see a therapist
Lots of questions asked
Unpleasant emotions
Arts and crafts too

Changes

You will change
It will be arranged

Don't be alarmed
You will not be harmed

It will be terrifying
There will be crying

But no more hiding
Then finally you will be flying

Medication

It's just a pill
Only for a small period of the day
It is in the routine of life now
Relying on it every day
But it will help me
Everyone needs some type of help
Medication is okay to take

Therapy

There's lots of talking
But also lots of helping
Keep a good attitude
To experience gratitude
So finally there can be healing

Writing Therapy

Express thoughts on paper
Allow it to flow out
Encourage others too
Find others with similar thoughts
Poems, journal, books, lyrics
There's many forms of writing
Choose the best for you

Friends

They saw behind the mask
They read between my lines
They wouldn't give up
They guided me through
Visited every day when hospitalized
Won't leave me be

Family

Supportive always
Understands I need time too
Love that never ends

Accepting

I can't allow this mental illness to stop me from living
I'm done just sitting

I'm ready to accept it
It's time to commit

To let the fear go
To let the emotions overflow

PART 2

You're Stronger Now to Succeed

Rainbow of Emotions

Blue is sadness becoming peace
Black is the color of depression growing into strength
Purple goes from tired to power
Gray turns loneliness to intelligence
Orange goes from helpless to determined
Red with anger to love
Green transforms jealousy to proud
Yellow transitions confusing into comfort
White goes from cold to newness

Depression

Blue: sad
Black: depressed
Gray: lonely
Red: angry
Orange: helpless
Purple: power
Green: jealous of others
Yellow: confused
White: cold

Happiness

Blue: peace
Red: love
Orange: determined
Purple: comfort
Green: proud
Yellow: comfort
Black: strength
Gray: intelligence
White: newness

Working on Me

This time is about me
I have to be first
In order to help others
I'm ready to be
As happy as I can

I took the first step
I can keep going
I might have a setback
But I won't let it stop me

I can focus on me

Scars

The wounds may heal
The scars may fade
But you will always remember

Yes, time will continue
But it still won't fade
Let it fuel you

You will live
The scars will stay
But it isn't a bad thing

It has made you, you
Don't try to erase them
Just let them be
Continue to remind yourself

Time

Healing cannot be rushed
You have to do it all
If you don't, you will be crushed
And you will fall

Take all the time you need
Others will understand
You will eventually succeed
Then you can finally stand

When that time comes
Be proud and loud
Hit the drums
And you will wow the crowd

Unfinished Story

Your story hasn't ended
It has been extended
It will continue and be splendid
Add to your story
It will be glory
The good, bad, and ugly will be blended

Not Your Only Trait

This mental illness doesn't define me
It isn't a problem with a simple fix
It's something I will work on
It's a small part of me
I will not give up
I will not lose this battle
Though I will have ups and downs
I can always get through
So throw me whatever
I am ready to fight
This mental illness isn't all of me
Take the time to learn other traits
You will be surprised by what you learn
I am able to support others too
I am a teacher with a kind heart
I have the patience to let others talk
I am the one ready with a helping hand
This mental illness doesn't define me
So please just accept me

Brain

The brain is tricky

Filled with lots of thoughts

Sometimes it helps

But sometimes not

All you have to do

Is practice new thoughts

To retrain your brain

So you can be happy

Tree

Growing and strong
  Always changing with something new
    Rising above to help yourself
      Helping others with protection and love
        Accepting help to be better

Fire

The flame may go down
But it isn't fully on the ground

Don't let it go out
Just give a shout

Someone will come along
To help you sing your song

Rising again
To your full potential is a win

Storm

The weather is changing
Dark clouds and thunder
The lightning strikes
The rain starts

Soon it quiets down
Now it all stops
       The sun is peeking through
       The clouds disappearing
The sun shines

The storm may come again
       But you'll be ready when it does
       You've won the battle before
So continue to remember you can again

Chameleon

Animals are special creatures
The chameleon has a neat feature

It will change its color
To hide from others

But sometimes it shines
To show it's fine

As you go through phases
Your mood changes

Emotions are meant to be released
So you can be freed

I want to be more than a chameleon

Believe

You need to believe
In order to achieve
And receive
Your dream
With help from the team
You can succeed

Look inside you
It's all there
Everything you need to do
To take care

Inspiring Others

Look at you go!
You have worked hard
You have pushed through
Now keep it up

Use your progress
To show others
It is possible
To overcome this

You may be the person
Whom someone else needs
To walk this path
And learn to live freely too

About the Author

Danielle Christy is a new author. She has personal experiences with mental-health issues. With the support of God, family, friends, and therapy, she is conquering these issues daily. Christy is a teacher residing in Ohio. She lives with her dog, Tilly.